Get Out!

Training Your Children to Leave the Nest

Lorene Price Henderson

Printed in the United States of America

First Edition, November 2018

ISBN: 9781730932465
Imprint: Independently published

For ordering bulk quantities, booking the author for speaking engagements,
as well as exploring other possibilities for collaboration, please email
Lorene.phenderson@simlohdynasty.com.

About the Author

An ordained minister, a missionary, a businesswoman, a leader, an innovator, mentor, and activist, Lorene Price Henderson is a woman of influence. With a history of life-changing events to reflect upon, Lorene Price Henderson is most noted for her ability to recognize potential, galvanize people, and strategize projects while producing maximum results.

With a heart for the hurting, Lorene Price Henderson has been leading impactful community efforts to address the educational, economic, social, and spiritual ills that burden communities. She has held several key working positions that have allowed her to accomplish this.

Lorene has worked in the juvenile justice system with over twenty years of experience (1993–2013) including St. Joseph Carondolet Child Care Services, Ada S. McKinley R.O.L.E. program, and Life Direction, a national organization that works in the public high schools and among adults, aged eighteen to thirty-five, to develop and nurture a hunger for positive values. Through the Cook County juvenile probation system, she was recognized for being one of the top community service providers in the Woodlawn Community.

Lorene was the founder and CEO of 2nd Chance Chicago NFP, an upscale resale boutique whose proceeds helped support her transitional home for homeless women. She served as the Evangelism Outreach Minister at New Beginnings Church of Chicago (Corey B. Brooks, Senior Pastor), which has a membership of over 2500 people, and oversaw outreach services and community programming. She served as the liaison between the church and community by providing biblical counseling and spiritual guidance.

Additionally, while working directly with the Office of the Mayor of Chicago, she was the lead organizer for the Project HOOD Walk Across America, a fifteen-mile march from Chicago's south side to Navy Pier with over 5000 people in attendance, bringing awareness to the excessive violence and senseless killings in Chicago. This event received local and national media attention. Both Governor Pat Quinn and Mayor Rahm Emanuel participated.

With an uncanny ability to navigate challenging circumstances, Lorene Price Henderson is a solution-based individual who leads with a firm and focused management style. Her track record of proven results has afforded her the opportunity to sit as a director for several organizations, offering wisdom and guidance.

Lorene also developed a new outreach training system for churches and community outreach initiatives called Creative Evangelism (CE). CE's mission is to teach those who are saved more creative, charismatic, and contemporary ways to introduce Christ to God's people through discipleship and outreach.

Born and raised in Chicago, Illinois, Lorene is married to Simeon Henderson and they have one child, Simeon Loren Henderson. The couple also raised Lorene's sister, Mariah Price. Lorene never fails to give all the glory to God for her accomplishments, and is strengthened daily by the biblical scriptures.

"Be careful not to practice your righteousness in front of others to be seen by them. If you do, you will have no reward from your Father in heaven" (Matthew 6:1, NIV).

What People are Saying about *Get Out!* and Lorene Price Henderson

This book is saturated with undeniable truth from personal experience. It acts as confirmation as others view me after I've been released from "the nest" because I am able to implement the things I've been taught. I am independent and I've never had so many epiphanies in my life.

—Mariah Price, sister, and child whom
God saw fit for Lorene to raise

Within minutes of reading Lorene's book, it immediately spoke to my heart. As a widow and mother of three children, this book has inspired me to have the tough conversations with myself and look at my parenting style as well as ways to improve it. It will also help so many families to get back to the basics as we prepare our children to leave the nest and become productive members of society. This book is filled with Lorene's personal and professional experiences that she gained on her journey, and I appreciate her for writing what was placed on her heart. *Get Out!* should definitely be in every learning institution and household.

—Regina Williams, mom of three and USN Veteran

Lorene has wholeheartedly dedicated herself to her craft of sowing with the best intention. We know that the measure you give will be the measure you get back, so how she has chosen to give is a reflection here of how important this truly is for her. She undeniably cares for the youth she has worked with and has inspired many of these young adults on all levels. Lorene has unceasingly encouraged me to pursue my own spiritual, personal, and professional goals. I believe she will undoubtedly empower many young adults to take this vital step forward.

—Elsie Guelespe, criminal justice agent

Mrs. Lorene Henderson is a phenomenal woman of God who loves the Lord with her whole heart. She is an extraordinary wife, mother, daughter, sister, evangelist, teacher, and my friend. Her book will give you insight and direction on how to help your child stand on their own and be as free as the birds. I wish her the absolute best in this journey.

—Reverend Dava Beckham

Lorene has been an inspiration, adviser, caregiver, leader, and motivator in all areas of social services. For the last thirteen years, she has completely morphed into a trailblazer, one who allows the world to gain knowledge from her journey! In this book, she gives a vivid picture of parenthood from her personal experiences. I'm honored to call this woman of god, daughter, wife, mother, and sister my friend! Now she will be known as a successful author, all to the glory of God!

—Minister Valerie Houston, music producer and songwriter

Lorene has been a mother even before having a child of her own. Ministering to youths in the juvenile system to women in the streets, she has not enabled the youth or ladies she has worked with but empowered them. With her social services experience and the call God has upon her life, she has the wisdom and tools to help parents' disciple their children and learn how to trust God that when you train up a child in the way he or she should go, then they will not depart.

—Margie R. Ivy

Get Out!
Training Your Children to Leave the Nest

Acknowledgments

I am grateful to God for trusting and allowing me to carry this book out to completion. This book is a result of me hearing God's voice and living out obedience is better than sacrifice.

The late Miles Monroe said, you should write about your passion, experience, testimony, revelation, obligation, and conviction. "If you don't write, you are a generational thief" (Miles Monroe). These thoughts alone encouraged me to document my ideas; to provide caretakers with guidance and assist them to train up a child--the next generation.

This book is dedicated to parents, caretakers, and mentors who God has entrusted His children with.

To Mariah, my sister/child, my baby girl who has made this book come to life by being a living testament of "Get Out".
To my son Simeon Loren, whom I will continue to apply these principles to.
To my loving and supportive husband, Simeon, who pressed me to "get it done".
To my Godmother Edie Cathey.
To my mother Laura and my late father James, who did their very best to raise me to love God with all my heart.

To my family and friends who pushed and prayed for me to write and complete the book. Those who read and critiqued the book and those who shared their experiences, I want to say thank you!

To my childhood mentors: Edward Madgett, and Roxanne Stevenson to name a few who influenced me to be the mentor and caretaker that I am today.

To parents who are struggling with releasing their adult child to embark on their journey to get out.

I pray that this book becomes a tool in raising the future.

Contents

Chapter 1
Survival

Guide to Parenting

"Start children off on the way they should go, and even when they are old they will not turn from it" (Proverbs 22:6, NIV). This scripture is the basis of the book: start children off the way you expect for them to go. The King James Version says, "Train up a child." This word, train, means to teach a particular skill or type of behavior through practice and instruction over a period of time. Train also means promotion. Christ-centered and Bible-based, the book can help in understanding that the word of God is and must be the foundation of being a parent. The definition of a parent is a caregiver of the offspring in their own species. In humans, a parent is the caretaker of a child.

There is a song by Miki Howard called "I'm in Love Under New Management." The very first part of the lyrics state, "Experience is a good teacher; it takes someone like me to know." I once handled parenting my way, meaning the way the world said it should be done. I have since started doing it God's way. During my season of being a single woman, I worked two full-time jobs in the social services spectrum. I have spent three years working in foster care, six years as a mentor for Cook County Juvenile Courts, and twelve years as a Juvenile Residential Treatment Specialist. During this time, I also housed children who were abandoned by their parents and owned and operated a transitional housing for young women and their small children (up to five years old). For ten years now, and still counting, I have been the guardian and parent of my sister, Mariah, who recently turned nineteen, and I'm blessed to be the biological parent of my five-year-old son, Simeon Loren.

This chapter is written for the parent and focuses on the personal process and areas within ourselves which we must examine first. The process will allow us to raise our children with the tools, principles, and life skills they will someday duplicate.

Trust the Process

"Trust in the Lord with all your heart and lean not on your own understanding; in all your ways, submit to him, and he will make your paths straight" (Proverbs 3:5–6, NIV). Trust is something positive. It is a real something, not a mere "happen-so" or "maybe-so." It is a definite attitude of soul and mind, a realization of our own need, and of God's sufficiency. It is the reaching out and anchoring of ourselves in God. There is no worry in trust. Our actions can cause delay. "All scripture is God-breathed and is useful for teaching, rebuking, correcting, and training in righteousness" (2 Timothy 3:16, NIV). If God said it, believe it. He says, "Be still, and know that I am God; I will be exalted among the nations, I will be exalted in the earth" (Psalm 46:10, NIV).

One of my own experiences was learning to trust the process. My father, who was dealing with lung cancer, informed me that he wanted to grant me guardianship of my sister, Mariah, who was seven years old at the time. I had no children of my own, and I knew I couldn't do it alone; so I prayed and asked God to guide me. He said, "Trust me in the process."

My mother has said, "How would you know if you don't try?" It wasn't an easy road, but ten years later, the fruits of trusting the process has paid off. As you read further in the book, I will expound more on my experiences with "trusting the process."

Pray and Fast

Fasting and prayer break the yoke of bondage and bring about a release of God's presence, power, and provision. Don't worry about anything; instead, pray about everything. Tell God what you need and thank him for all he has done. You will then experience God's peace, which exceeds anything we can understand. "His peace will guard your hearts and minds as you live in Christ Jesus" (Philippians 3:6–7, NLT). Now, parents, I know it's probably second nature to you to worry, especially if your child is sick or you are going through financial troubles or your child's behavior is not aligning with what you taught him or her. Worrying is a human characteristic. Oftentimes, after we've done all we can do to prevent a bad outcome, we can't eliminate the possibility that something could go wrong. But when we fast and pray, God promises his peace.

Repent

This means confessing that the way I have done something is not correct and must be changed. The Bible also tells us that true repentance will result in a change of action (Luke 3:8–14; Acts 3:19). Acts 26:20 declares, "I preached that they should repent and turn to God and prove their repentance by their deeds." What is this saying? Repentance is a change of mind that results in a change of actions. If you know what you've been doing is not working or is not right, repent and change it.

At first glance, it may be hard for you to find the connection between parenting and repenting. But sometimes in raising a child, there are certain practices that you realize aren't working, such as beating or cussing out your child(ren) or calling them everything but a child of God. You may realize that you are disciplining them in ways that you don't want them passing down and using on their own children. Maybe what you first thought would help is actually doing more damage to them. That's when you decide to repent and change your mind. It will consequently result in a change of actions.

"Forgive yourself and forgive others" (Isaiah 43:18). Forget the former things. In this book, I need for you to first forgive yourself for past and present parenting mistakes made while raising your children. Forgive others as well, including your own parents, spouse, baby daddy, or baby momma and children. Forgive, stop feeling angry or resentful toward someone for an offense, flaw, or mistake. We all make them, and God has forgiven you. No, it's not easy, but it's a must! Jesus said, "Father, forgive them for they do not know what they are doing" (Luke 23:34a, NIV). This sounds like us talking to God about our children.

When my parents separated, I made the decision that I would never get married and have children, because I saw my mother stressed, angry, and hurt; and whatever she felt was displayed in her actions. I also know I wasn't the easiest child to deal with. I was also stressed, angry, and hurt about their separation. I entered an even darker space after being sexually assaulted by my doctor, and I was angry when my father didn't believe me. My father was the first man I ever loved, and I expected him to avenge this horrific act. I was his baby girl, and he promised to always protect me. I struggled with those things and carried this burden inside until I got older and realized that people have issues going on in their own lives.

I realized that I had to forgive that doctor and my father for not responding as I thought he should. Trials and tribulations can come unexpectedly, and they can turn your life upside down. I realized that in order to go on with my life, I had to forgive my parents and understand that their issues, along with having a family, is a balancing act. Now that I'm a wife and a mother myself, I can relate to their experiences, although I didn't understand at the time. My mother and I now have a great relationship, and because I forgave my father, I was able to raise his daughter, who is my step-sister, as my own after he passed away.

You should forgive because it releases you from the pressures of the past. It's not enough to say you forgive someone. Your actions, thoughts, and attitudes should also reflect it.

At all costs, avoid having hang-ups about how you were parented to the point that it prevents you from being an effective parent. The same holds true for any other part of your life you may have issues with, such as a toxic or hostile relationship between a man and the mother of his child or your regrets for not raising your kids from a previous marriage the way they should be raised. Do not let any of that hinder you from practicing the right way of parenting to the children you have now. You must also be in a position to forgive yourself. In all of the above situations, practicing forgiveness may be a challenge, but it can and should be done.

Breaking Generational Curses

"A hemorrhaging generation cannot produce a healthy generation" (T. D. Jakes). In the Old Testament, a generational curse was a consequence for a specific nation (Israel) for a specific sin (idolatry). The effects of sin are naturally passed down from one generation to the next. When a parent has a sinful lifestyle, their children are likely to practice the same sinful lifestyle. The warning in Exodus 20:5 is the fact that the children will choose to repeat the sins of their fathers. The cure for generational curses has always been repentance. When Israel turned from idols to serve the living God, the "curse" was broken and God saved them (Judges 3:9, 15; 1 Samuel 12:10–11). The cure for a "generational curse" is repentance of the sin in question, faith in Christ, and a life consecrated to the Lord. According to Romans 12:1–2, ESV, "I appeal to you therefore, brothers, by the mercies of God, to present your bodies as a living sacrifice, holy and acceptable to God, which is your spiritual worship. Do not be conformed to this world, but be transformed by the renewal of your mind."

You should be praying that the family curses be no longer in the lives of you and your seed/child.

I'm going to keep it real and be straightforward with you. When my husband and I got married and pregnant right away, we sat down and discussed all of the sinful lifestyles that we noticed being practiced either on his side of the family or mine, and we agreed we didn't want Mariah or our future child to be exposed to or learn to emulate these behaviors. We vowed that we would do our best to not fall into that kind of life nor allow anyone to expose sinful habits around our children. This isn't to say my husband and I were being judgmental, but we were merely doing what we could to break the generational curse and raise our children to fear God.

Each day, we resolve that living a life of sin is a thing of our past and thank God for Jesus and seek to keep a relationship with him. I'm not saying that you won't sin, but as followers of

Christ, you should not practice sin. The Bible says, "For all have sinned; and come short of the glory of God" (Romans 3:23, KJV). The Bible also says, in 2 Chronicles 7:14, ESV, "If my people, who are called by my name, will humble themselves and pray and seek my face and turn from their wicked ways, then will I hear from heaven, and I will forgive their sin and will heal their land."

Examples of generational curses or "sinful lifestyles" can be found in a number of scriptures including being wicked, immoral, evil, corrupt, disrespectful; or being an alcoholic, food-glutton, an addict to sex, drugs, and money (Ephesians 5:18; Proverbs 23:20–30; 1 John 3:8; 1 Timothy 6:10).

There are many people in this world who don't think this is a big deal or think that those sinful practices are actually burdening them; but ask yourself, do you really want your children to experience the same things that caused you pain and heartache? We realize they will have troubles, but as parents, we want to minimize these problems by introducing them to a better way—Jesus Christ.

Be Patient

"Do not be anxious about anything, but in every situation, by prayer and petition, with thanksgiving, present your requests to God" (Philippians 4:6, NIV). It won't always happen overnight, but always remember that the word of God says, "Love is patient and love is kind. It does not envy, it does not boast, it is not proud" (1 Corinthians 13:4, NIV). To be patient is to love, and to love is to be patient.

When Mariah turned sixteen and was fully experiencing puberty, her hormones started really kicking in, and it seemed as if all hell had broken loose. It didn't matter what I had taught her, how I had warned her, or what she had personally witnessed; when puberty struck, it struck hard, and it seemed that everything I was trying to protect her from happened.

I know someone is saying, what is the puberty stage? Puberty is when the brain triggers the production of the sex hormones. I felt that the eight years she had been with me was wasted and that she had not just failed me, but I had failed her. In my anger, I sent her to her biological mother that summer. And might I say because I had lost my patience, I unwittingly sent her to a place that wasn't safe, a place that would allow the puberty stage to become even more tainted. I did this because I had run out of patience. So I thought!

I was angry, disappointed, kept records of wrongs, and felt betrayed. One day, I was sitting and studying the word of God, and he reminded me, "Love is patient, love is kind. It does not envy, it does not boast, it is not proud. It does not dishonor others, it is not self-seeking, it is not easily angered, it keeps no record of wrongs. Love does not delight in evil but rejoices with the truth. It always protects, always trusts, always hopes, always perseveres" (1 Corinthian 13:4–7, NIV).

I went and got Mariah and told her I loved her too much to put her in an environment that could be detrimental to her. I promised God and Mariah to be patient through the process. I also promised that I would discipline her and love the hell out of her.

Friends, I must admit that practicing this principle was difficult then, and it's still difficult, but the rewards are great. It all paid off. With prayer and fasting, all things worked out for Mariah's good. Now I'm still practicing this principle as I raise my son.

Seek Wisdom

"Heavenly wisdom creates a wise heart" (James 3:17). Seek God starting from the day of conception, delivery, foster care, adoption, or guardianship. Seek the wisdom of others. Parents need God's wisdom on how to do the job effectively; this includes the work of rearing our children properly. As parents, we can also seek the scientific knowledge of how to train up a child. We've heard of the adage, "It takes a village to raise a child."

Other parents, child mentors, and counselors experience accomplishments and failures; we can pull all that wisdom together to contribute to the rearing of each child we deal with, no matter how briefly. Our collective gifts of nurturing can assist the process. If you do not have children at home, then perhaps you can be used by God to share these principles with those who do.

I birthed my son at the age of forty. I had been working, mentoring, and providing safe havens for children while also counseling parents and their children twenty years before I had my son. Maybe you are also in a season without children; however, it should not stop you from sharing wisdom with people who do have children. Not having children does not mean you do not have wisdom and the ability to assist others. People have often said because I did not have children, I was not in the position to help them with parenting. This did not negate that I had godly wisdom to share. Obtain His wisdom, and share it as He leads you.

What is the goal? Understand that your goals may not be the children's future goals. You may have some goals pertaining to your child's career, such as to be a doctor, a lawyer, to go to college, to own their own business, or even become the President of the USA; but there should also be some biblical parenting goals. For example, refer to Steve Cole's *Ten Key Principles*:

1. Protection and correction is our duty; this is what sheltering is.

2. "Spare the rod, spoil the child" (Proverbs 13:24).

3. Your child is an assignment sent by God.

4. Build character.

Instead of building cosmetics of a person or child, you are to build their character; that is, the fruit of the Holy Spirit within them. You are your child's caretaker physically and emotionally. You are a counselor and confidante; you are in a good position to give sound advice, Biblical advice, to encourage your child to reach for the stars to seek God in all things.

I hear you asking, "How do I do that? How do you teach what you don't know?" The manual has been written and it is the Bible, the Word of God. Always remember that you are the first teacher. You teach them the difference between right and wrong, how to conduct themselves in social settings, and everything in between. A parent's job, as a teacher, is never-ending.

My mother has been and continues to be available for my sister and I mentally, physically, spiritually and, yes, financially; however, there are expectations and goals attached. You are a role model. Children imitate their parents' behavior just as we should imitate God.

"Dear friend, do not imitate what is evil but what is good. Anyone who does what is good is from God. Anyone who does what is evil has not seen God" (3 John 1:11, NIV). Last but not least, you want to train them up to "get out!" The goal is to raise competent and capable adults.

Notes

What scriptures or principles stood out in this chapter?

_____

_____

_____

_____

_____

_____

What will I do to prepare myself and or children as it relates to this chapter?

_____

_____

_____

_____

_____

_____

My prayer is.....

_____

_____

_____

_____

_____

_____

_____

_____

Chapter 2
Expose

It Starts in the Womb

"For you created my inmost being; you knit me together in my mother's womb" (Psalm 139:13, 432 NIV). The gospel of Jesus starts in the womb. You are the first preacher they will hear, and this includes talking, praying, reading, and listening to music. Why is this important? Psalm 58:3, NIV, "Even from birth the wicked go astray; from the womb they are wayward, spreading lies." We have noticed that people let their children listen to Beethoven and Mozart, thinking it will make them smart. We know that listening to the things of God will help them become spiritual. "So faith comes by hearing, and hearing the Word of God" (Romans 10:17 EVS).

The womb creates a safe place. The womb I'm referring to here is the home or nest—a sacred place. As parents, we should provide an environment that is safe, full of mercy, and filled with peace. God has trusted us with his dear children. We are to plant seeds that will produce fruit. We are the ones who will teach, water, and maintain the direction in which they will grow. We should always strive to provide womb care while they're in our custody. If you are unfamiliar with what seeds and fruits I am referring to, read further and I will explain them more fully in the next parts.

The Word Brings Salvation (Life)

Romans 10:14, "How, then, can they call on the one they have not believed in? And how can they believe in the one of whom they have not heard? And how can they hear without someone preaching to them?" (NIV).

What they hear is who they become. We must become active doers of the Word, the truth that Christ Jesus reveals to us.

James 1:22, "But be ye doers of the word, and not hearers only."

Purpose and Gifts

"And you must love the Lord your God with all your heart, all your soul, all your mind, and all your strength" (Mark 12:30, NIV). We must teach our children that they must love God and his people, and that Jesus is our savior. In order for our children to learn their purpose and gifts, we must expose them to Jesus and the word of the Lord. How do we do that? There are many ways, such as one-on-one teaching at home as well as being an example of the word by applying it to our lives. Christian social media platforms, Christian TV networks, Christian Bible apps for children and teens are also available. And lastly, attending a church or place of worship that is Christ-centered and Bible-based, a place where you can be taught/discipled on the things of Christ.

The Bible tells us we need to have Christian fellowship so we can worship God with other believers and be taught his word for our spiritual growth (Acts 2:42; Hebrews 10:25). Fellowship is the place where believers can love one another (1 John 4:12), encourage one another (Hebrews 3:13), serve one another

(Galatians 5:13), instruct one another (Romans 15:14), honor one another (Romans 12:10), and be kind and compassionate to one another (Ephesians 4:32).

Let me make it clear: going to church and being around other believers doesn't make you a Christian; however, if you are a true Christian, you will have a desire to be around other believers on a regular basis.

"Without the God-given habit of corporate worship and the God-given mandate of corporate accountability, we will not prove faithful over the long haul" (Kevin DeYoung).

Fruit of the Spirit

"But the fruit of the Spirit is love, joy, peace, forbearance, kindness, goodness, faithfulness, gentleness and self-control. Against such things there is no law" (Galatians 5:22–23, NIV). Wow! The first thing we learn here is love and what it takes to acquire the fruit, which is gentleness and self-control. Those attributes described as the fruit of the Spirit work hand in hand; they all complement one another.

Teach how to love and nurture. "Owe no man anything, but to love one another, for he that loveth another hath fulfilled the law" (Romans 3:8, KJV).

Plant the Seed

It is our job to make sure they get water and sunshine; it all starts in the womb, which is at home, in the nest or in the nursery. In this context, the nursery is an institution or environment in which certain types of people or qualities are fostered or bred. When my son, Simeon Loren, was around two years old, I started a garden, and Loren—as we call him—had an opportunity to assist me with the nursery where the garden would be for all of the different kinds of veggies that were going to grow there. The first thing I taught him was how to plant the seeds in the soil and how delicate he had to be when covering the seeds with the dirt. The next thing I taught him was how it required his time; he had to spend each day watering and caring for the garden. In the end, he enjoyed watching it grow, and he enjoyed the "fruits and vegetables" of his labor.

Just as I taught Loren about caring for the seeds we planted, as parents, we are responsible for showing our children how to love and care for things given to them. This too can begin by teaching them how to treat their toys and personal belongings with love and care. In return, they will treat the belongings of others with love. This will transcend into their love for people, which is a testament to how parents nurture their children. My son is such a loving boy that people enjoy having him around.

Love God and his people. Love God because he first loved us. "A new command I give you: Love one another. As I have loved you, so you must love one another. By this everyone will know that you are my disciples, if you love one another" (John 13:34–35, NIV).

Plant the Seed and it will Grow

I knew I had to saturate Mariah with the word of God so I made the decision to take her out of the public school she had attended and put her in a Christian Bible-based, Bible-believing grade school. When it was time for her to choose a college—a place of freedom—Mariah chose a very conservative Christian institution. When I asked her why she chose that college, she reminded me that it was the first college she had visited while attending the Christian grade school, and her principal at that time had attended that college. Mariah was in the sixth grade when she visited that school, and the seed that was planted had obviously left a lasting impression. Again I say, "Plant the seed!"

We must Remember the Scripture

"For God so loved the world that he gave his one and only Son, that whoever believes in him shall not perish but have eternal life" (John 3:16, NIV). That's another "wow" moment right there. I personally couldn't imagine giving up my son or his life for this world. Since God loved us so much, we must love his people. Love is an action word! We should go out of our way to express or display some type of love action. The Bible also teaches us, "Whoever claims to love God yet hates a brother or sister is a liar. For whoever does not love their brother and sister, whom they have seen, cannot love God, whom they have not seen" (1 John 4:20, NIV).

Giving and Sharing

You must each decide in your heart how much to give. And don't give reluctantly or in response to pressure. "For God loves a person who gives cheerfully" (2 Corinthians 9:7, NLT). Don't be stingy! Some may say that kids naturally have a giving heart. Well, I beg to differ; when they hit the toddler age, they begin to have issues sharing their toys with other kids. They must be taught to share and give to others. We can't allow them to take their toys and go home. We must encourage them to share and give to children less fortunate. So many times, our children have more toys than they are able to play with. We must continuously train them to be unselfish in giving and sharing with others.

One day, while I was outside with Loren as he was playing with his action figure, we saw a little boy, and the two of them began playing with the toy. As we were leaving and Loren was taking his toy with him, the other boy began crying. I saw this as a teachable moment and suggested to Loren to let the little boy have the toy. I explained to my son that he had other toys at home to play with, and it appeared the little boy really liked the action figure. With little reluctance, Loren decided to give the toy to the little boy. Later, when we discussed the event, Loren was happy that he gave the toy away. He learned that sharing can bring happiness.

Nurture your Kid's Calling

Hang in there, the fruit will become sweet. Just as it takes time for the fruit to mature, it will also take time and patience for your child's calling to be realized. When we speak of the child's calling, we are referring to who God wants them to become. We must spend time cultivating their calling. Most of the time, what we see as parents is just a mere glimpse of the calling that is on our children. Just as we planted and nurtured the garden, it is our responsibility to water the calling on our children through encouragement and continued prayer. We realize we must continue to give them Jesus and let God do the work.

People, Places, and Things

Expose your children to as many meaningful experiences as possible. Take time to introduce them to different cultures and people. We must teach our children cultural diversity. Heaven will be filled with people from all ethnicities and backgrounds.

Take your children to different places, i.e. restaurants, museums, lakes, parks, mountains. Expose them to city life if you're from the country. If you live in the city, take your kids to the country or the suburbs. I can remember when I was a kid, around seven, taking a ferry from Detroit to Boblo Island in Canada. The intriguing and ivy-covered Boblo Island and all the great amusement rides are treasured memories to me. My family also took road trips down south to Arkansas to visit my grandparents. In my eyes, the house was the size of a shack or, as my mom would say, a shotgun house. They called it shotgun house, because if you fired a bullet through the front door it would go out the backdoor without hitting a wall. I was growing up in the city and had never seen a house that small.

My sister and I also went to North Carolina to visit my Aunt Lynn's when I was around five. This was the first trip we made without our parents. My first plane trip was to Colorado after I had graduated from the eighth grade. I remember seeing the dark rolling mountains in Colorado and crossing over the Royal Gorge Bridge. To this day, I still love to travel because my parents made sure we knew there was more to God's great creation than our hometown of Chicago.

For a Chicago native like me, accustomed to the noises of police sirens at odd hours of night, the serene evenings in Arkansas punctuated by the sounds of birds and the creek flowing behind my grandparents' house were life-changing. They have become as much a part of me as my city upbringing, so much so that I eventually moved to the south years later.

What are other things you can expose your children to? Sports, music, learning to play an instrument(s), travel, science, the arts, drama, or acting. Exploring these things assisted in the development of who I am today. My mother would call me a "jack of all trades" because to this day, I will try almost anything. My mind, body, and spirit learned to adapt to change. Whether that change was good, bad, holy, and not so holy, my experiences helped me become the godly woman that I am today.

Notes

What scriptures or principles stood out in this chapter?

_____

_____

_____

_____

_____

_____

_____

What will I do to prepare myself and or children as it relates to this chapter?

_____

_____

_____

_____

_____

_____

_____

My prayer is.....

_____

_____

_____

_____

_____

_____

_____

_____

Chapter 3
Creating Independence

Work Smarter, Not Harder

Parent on purpose; this will build the necessary life skills in our kids. How can we raise competent adults if we're always doing everything for our children? Of course, I'm speaking about age-appropriate chores and responsibilities. If you need to know at what age you should start specific chores, Google it; there is a ton of information out there. Cleaning their rooms and doing chores around the house will teach them how to appreciate their surroundings and personal property. It will also get them in the path of learning to maintain their space when they are out renting or owning their own home in the future.

My son was taught to clean and organize his room at around three and a half years old. While taking a tour at the daycare provider's house, I noticed that the children were putting away the toys and separating them into individual containers. Blocks, animal toys, dolls, puzzles, and costumes all had their own proper place. When I got home, I started doing the same thing. I personally feel that if a child can operate a cell phone, then they can learn how to do some type of chore. Tell them to Google how to clean. My son could not read when he started using my cell phone. One day, I heard him telling the phone what to pull up on the screen, and I could not believe it. Children nowadays are literally coming out the womb learning how to operate cell phones.

Show them how to wash their clothes and put them away in their proper places. Make them understand that it's not a good practice to leave them on the floor with clean clothes mixed with dirty clothes.

They should learn how to prepare their own lunches. Tell them, "If you don't prepare and pack it, you don't eat." I did not say they had to buy it; it's my job to make sure the food is in the house. They should learn how to prepare and pack simple meals. When my family plans outings to the park, beach, or amusement parks, I inform the children they must assist in packing things that will be needed. I had been trying to teach Mariah how to cook for years, she just did not have the desire to cook, and because I like my food cooked with love, I didn't need for her to cook for me. Don't get me wrong; she was in the kitchen helping as my sous chef. They may not cook, but they will work for that meal. I would often say to her that I would not always be there to cook for her. The day Mariah turned eighteen and had graduated from high school was the last time I cooked for her. Then one day, I got a call from her in college asking me how to make baked mac and cheese. I laughed and gave her the recipe, but said the meal would have been better if she had practiced earlier.

You are not an Alarm Clock

Waking your kids or teens up is not your job; that is what the alarm clock is for. I need extra minutes for myself. Parents wake up early to wake up their kids. Really? When I'm ready, you need to be ready! I should not and I will not wait on you. And if I have to wait, there will be consequences, especially if it affects me and my schedule. It will teach your child how to prepare and how to manage their time. When they are in school and the school bell rings for the next class, will you be there to say it's time for them to go to the next class? No! Teach them early to have a sense of urgency. One day, they will be accountable and on someone else's clock.

Teach your children how to fill out their own forms such as trip slips. If they can read and write, then they can sign their name. By the time it gets to me, it should be filled out, and all I have to do is sign it. When Mariah and I would go to the doctor's office, at every visit, they would give us that long medical history form to fill out. I would give it to her to fill out, and if she had any questions, I would give her the answer. She is nineteen now and has known for a while how to fill out documents. That task is not foreign to her. It has also allowed her to learn some things about herself that she would otherwise not find out if she had someone else constantly filling out forms for her. She is now in college completing all of her paperwork for school and classes. She is not calling me constantly asking me how-to questions.

Accepting Consequences

You shouldn't treat their failure to plan as your personal emergency. School projects do not get assigned the night before they are due. Therefore, I do not run out and pick up materials at the last minute to get a project finished. You should always keep school supplies and general materials on hand for the procrastinating child. As for other project-specific items, they will have to inform you they need them in advance as soon as the project is assigned, not the day before the deadline. Do not race to Walmart for your kid who hasn't taken the time to plan.

My biggest pet peeve is seeing parents run back and forth to the school because the child left something they needed, such as a homework or a science project, after-school necessities like football or basketball shoes, or a musical instrument, and they don't want to have to deal with the consequences that the school may have for them. But I bet you those kids won't forget that cell phone. You can use it as a starting point: Tell your child to use that cell phone, tablet, or device and save it on their calendar, tasks, or things-to-do apps—and set the alarm!

Preparing for college is not a foreign notion in our house. The processes and the things to expect along the way were introduced around seventh grade and continuously brought up all through high school. We explained to Mariah that maintaining good grades, qualifying for scholarships, and communicating with potential colleges were her job, not ours. Our job was to coach her in making the right choices and to hold her accountable with handling her business. We also explained the possible consequences if she didn't take care of the things she should. Mariah is now in college and she is experiencing both the negative and positive effects of preparation and being proactive.

Giving and Receiving (i.e. Birthdays, Holidays, Thank-You Cards or even just Saying Thank you)

This works both ways. When my son turned four, I realized he would start requesting particular birthday gifts, and for an entire year, he would talk about what he wanted to do for the next birthday. He was learning how to receive, but I also needed him to learn how to be a giver. Since Loren turned six years old in February, I told him Mommy's birthday is in September and that he has seven months to work on getting me a gift. It could be something simple as a flower he picked from our yard. What matters is he learned how to be a giver.

As for our teenager, she started learning around the age of thirteen that if you don't give, you won't receive! We stopped accepting the cute little school-made heart cards because we were giving her money every now and then and she could save to purchase a $1 card. We have to teach our children how to be givers and not just be recipients.

"Give, and you will receive. Your gift will return to you in full: pressed down, shaken together to make room for more, running over, and poured onto your lap. The amount you give will determine the amount you get back," (Luke 6:38, NLV). You are to teach your children to use the way you give, and the way God gives is their guide on how they themselves should give. Giving exhibits God's heart. I know they're not able to match the monetary cost of what you give, but at least they should give and give from the heart.

"Remember this whoever sows sparingly will also reap sparingly, and whoever sows generously will reap generously" (2 Corinthians 9:6–7, NIV). When you give and don't teach your children to give, you are raising selfish, "all-about-me" children who turn into selfish, "all-about-me" adults.

Sheltering your Child

Your child will either love you or hate you for this. Some people will say that sheltering is cruel, that it is dooming them to be ignorant or naive to people, places, and the things of this world. Others may say if you don't shelter your children, you are letting society raise them, making them wander too far from the nest. Some also view sheltering as not letting your child learn, explore, or play unless you as a parent agree with the process of how your child does those things.

My husband and I are very guilty of sheltering our children. You don't judge me, and I won't judge you! Pray for us as we pray for you to right a wrong and if what we are doing is excessive and harmful to our children.

I will break down three sheltering areas in which parents shelter their children.

Possessive Sheltering
The Abuse of Over-parenting

Like I said before, I will not be judging anyone. Over-parenting or being possessive is sometimes referred to as helicopter parenting, hyper-protective parenting, or "it's-my-way-or-no-way" parenting. The helicopter parent is one who knows their child's every move and vigilantly monitors the child. My husband and I have memberships to a gym, and the gym has a play area for children to attend while their parents work out. Simeon and I would take turns checking on our son Loren who was four years old at the time. At the end of the workout, we would pick up Loren. I informed the caregiver that we were grateful for them and that we hoped we didn't bother them too much by checking in on our son. The attendant responded that all was well and that we were not a bother, and that they were used to helicopter parents.

If a child with hyper-protective parents so much as coughs, sneezes, or gets a paper cut, they are rushed to the emergency room. The "it's-my-way-or-no-way" parent can be the overly controlling and religious parent who will not bend or display grace or mercy with their child. Everything has to be black and white.

Preventive Sheltering

This is when a child is not allowed to fend for him or herself, not being able to function physically, financially, or mentally without his or her parents. I was talking to a friend of mine one day about the way she had been raised. With no hesitation, she said to me that she was "sheltered as a child." When I asked her what she meant, she went on to explain that her parents took care of everything, so much so that even after she left home, they were still trying to take care of her affairs. She eventually figured out how to make it on her own, but it was not an easy task. She went on to say how important it is to teach and allow children to try things and make mistakes in order for you as the parent to use the mistakes as a learning opportunity.

Let's look at another scenario. My cousin, a parent of a high school student, was driving him to school. Before letting him out the car, my cousin asked her son some questions:

Do you have your pencils?

Do you have your gym clothes?

Do you have your money?

Do you have your homework?

Do you have your blue notebook?

Do you have your instrument?

Do you have this?

Do you have that?

My question is, what is the priority on this list that affects the parent? Do you have your money to get home? Why? Because if he didn't have the money to get home, it would cause the parent to be inconvenienced. Everything else would have a consequence for the teenager and not the parent, which would teach the teenager more responsibility.

Protective Sheltering

Parents are naturally protective. "By faith, Moses, when he was born, was hidden (protected) for three months by his parents, because they saw that the child was beautiful and they were not afraid of the king's edict" (Hebrews 11:23, ESV). Parents are often guilty of sheltering their children to an extent, but at the end of the day, understand that there's a thin line between love and hate. As parents, we do not want the pendulum to swing between love and hate. Instead, we want to establish a balance. Make sure your sheltering is out of love for them and not out of your unwillingness to relinquish control.

Teach them how to Study God's Word

The Lord's prayer is a basic and very important pattern as Jesus taught us to pray when the disciples asked. Given by Jesus in Matthew 6:9–14 ("This is how you should pray," he said), it is considered an outline of an individual Christian's relationship with God and other people.

"Pray then like this: 'Our Father in heaven, hallowed be your name. Your kingdom come, your will be done, on earth as it is in heaven. Give us this day our daily bread, and forgive us our debts, as we also have forgiven our debtors. And lead us not into temptation, but deliver us from evil. For thy is the kingdom and the power forever and ever. Amen'" (Matthew 6:9–13, NLV)!

There are all kinds of Bibles and Bible tools for people of all ages. I have been introducing my son to the word of God since he was in the womb. The moment Mariah moved in with me at the age of nine, I started pouring the word of God into her spirit. "Do your best to present (study) yourself to God as one approved, a worker who does not need to be ashamed and who correctly handles the word of truth" (2 Timothy 2:15, NIV). Study so you will be well-equipped.

The Armor of God

"Finally, be strong in the Lord and his mighty power. Put on the full armor of God, so that you can take your stand against the devil's schemes" (Ephesians 6:10, NIV).

Now that Mariah is away at college, I'm not worried because I know that she is well-equipped with the word of God. When she gets sick, she can pray for healing. When she is stressed, she can pray for God's peace; and when she is confused and full of doubt, she can pray for provision. That's what it means to train up a child—to give them God's word and let him do the work in them.

Notes

What scriptures or principles stood out in this chapter?

_____

_____

_____

_____

_____

_____

What will I do to prepare myself and or children as it relates to this chapter?

_____

_____

_____

_____

_____

_____

_____

My prayer is.....

_____

_____

_____

_____

_____

_____

_____

_____

Chapter 4
Generational Changes

I have given them your word and the world has hated them, for they are not of the world any more than I am of the world. My prayer is not that you take them out of the world but that you protect them from the evil one.

—John 17: 14–15, NIV 776

I have come to notice that we "new day parents," as some call us, concentrate more on working for the material things of this world or how we can accommodate what the child wants instead of what they need. We should be working on the spiritual, mental, emotional, and physical well-being of our children. As the scripture says, we must protect them from the evil one. We must evaluate, teach, and make better and conscious decisions. The children we are raising are our "future." I must admit that when I take time to observe what is going on with our children, I find it to be quite disturbing.

R-E-S-P-E-C-T

"Honor your father and your mother, so that you may live long in the land the LORD your God is giving you" (Exodus 20:12, NIV). Honor is giving respect not only for merit, but also for rank. You must respect leadership or authority, even though you might not always agree. Similarly, children of all ages should honor their parents, regardless of whether or not their parents "deserve" honor.

"Honor them with both actions and attitudes... Honor their unspoken as well as spoken wishes."

—Rev. Tony Raker

A wise son heeds his father's instruction, but a mocker does not listen to rebuke. (Proverbs 13:1)

The Bible says we must teach good. What worked for you might just work for them. Something as simple as saying, "Yes, sir" and "Yes, ma'am." I know a lot of people who did not grow up this way, but one of the things I have noticed and that we cannot get away from is when we are in the presence of people with authority. The protocol is to address them with their title, such as "Yes or no, Your Honor," or "Yes, officer."

My son has been saying "Yes, ma'am" and "Yes, sir," since he could talk. When he was a toddler, we came across some people who would say, "Oh, that is cute, but he doesn't have to say that to me. It makes me feel old."

Other people would commend him for being so respectful. If you're not that parent, then at least have them say yes and no. We must inform our children that we are not their equals, and honestly, we will never be.

Make Your Kids Accountable so that Accountability to Others Won't Be a Problem

One of the most dangerous things parents indirectly teach their children is to disrespect authority. How is this so? Well, when a child is disrespectful to you and there are no boundaries within the household, children grow up to display the same behavior with people of authority—their teachers, bosses on the job, their elders, and their neighbors. Gone are the days when a neighbor saw a child doing wrong and could correct or stop the child's negative behavior. These days, you will be fussed at by the children and their parents. We must remember that it takes a village. This proverb means that it takes an entire community to raise a child. A child gets greater chances of becoming a healthy adult if the entire community takes an active role in contributing to his or her rearing.

Don't Parent out of Guilt

Don't allow your children to do or have certain things too early just because you didn't have those things or were told you couldn't have them when you were a child; or just because other kids are doing it, such as wearing provocative hairstyles and clothes, using makeup, dating, watching certain TV shows, driving cars, and hosting or attending fancy, over-the-top parties.

When we were children, we would say, "Can we do different things?" And in an attempt to make our parents feel guilty, we would say, "Mary is doing the thing we wanted to do;" or "Mary is having a party;" or "Mary is going downtown on the bus."

My mother's response would be, "I'm not Mary's mother, I'm yours!" And that would be the end of the conversation.

This generation of parents allow their children to manipulate and control them, and consequently, they don't teach their children how to survive in this world of "I can have anything and everything." So they think! What you start, the child thinks you must finish and always do. Sometimes I wonder who is the parent. This is what I call "you owe me," and I will talk about this later in Chapter 5.

How you raise your children is how your children will take care of you. Teach love, and love will return to you. Honoring parents is the only command in scripture that promises long life as a reward. Those who honor their parents are blessed (Jeremiah 35:18–19). In contrast, those who have depraved minds and exhibit ungodliness in the last days are characterized by disobedience to parents (Romans 1:30; 2 Timothy 3:2). Someone could say, "But I did raise them to love and care for others, but they're grown now, and I don't know what went wrong." What happened is that they chose disobedience. It's not your fault, but you need to know that you don't have to accept disobedient behavior.

Spend Time, not Money

Be intentional about parenting. It requires patience, love, understanding, and your time. Not money! Children are happier with your presence than they are with your presents. When Mariah was younger, we had a lot of game nights and spent a lot of time talking. It wasn't just about playing the games, but we got to know one another better; and as time passed, the things we learned about each other made our bond stronger.

As for my own childhood, taking trips, playing in the park, helping my father fix cars, having our parents present at all the events my sister and I had are the things I remember and miss the most. My son always tells his dad not to go to work today. And his dad's responds, "I have to go so I can pay bills and buy you stuff."

Loren will then say, "I don't want the stuff, Dad; I want you." Loren loves to be in the presence of his parents. Spending time and being involved with your children are things you just can't put a price on.

Inspector Gadget

Inspector Gadget is the world's first bionic policeman. He was the main character in an animated science fiction television series. The bumbling detective is equipped with an incredible array of gadgets to help him in his never-ending battles against crime and corruption. As parents, we must be like Inspector Gadget and understand that it is a never-ending battle against protecting your children from the evil one or things of this world.

I Own it All

Check everything, including the space you allow them to occupy. It is *my* room in *my* house. The parent should check all electronic devices no matter who pays the bill. If they live under your roof or in your nest, then feel free and secure to check when you want to.

I remember when Mariah received a cell phone from her biological mother. I informed her mother that no matter who bought the phone, it was in my house and I would check it whenever I felt like it; and if there was any inappropriate use, the phone would be returned or destroyed. My house, my rules.

Mobile App Locator/GPS

I know some of you are saying that this is too much. Well, I didn't invent the apps, someone else did. It's not always about if you trust your kids; it is also about safety and security and the fact that kids these days are not as responsible as they once were.

Education: Intentionally Versus Actively

Parents need to be involved in the activities and the academics. You are still responsible for coaching your children along the way. Helping with homework, doing drills to prep for exams, monitoring grades, and helping with fundraisers—this is what I call being an intentional parent about education and school. You are merely active, but not intentional, when you are there for all of the rewards but did not assist in the intentional need of the children. Being an intentional parent, you are not just there when the child receives honors from school or have a school performance. The intentional parents help the child prepare or manage his time better to be ready for school and the performances. I have noticed that schools now are requiring parents to be involved in their children's school affairs, serving a minimum of forty hours a year of community service.

Life Skills
Prodigal Son—Wasteful (Luke 15:11–32)

Teach how to go after what they want, how to survive, or how to become an entrepreneur by putting up a lemonade stand, washing cars, mowing lawns, doing hair, babysitting, having a bake sale, or being a paperboy. Who made the rule that we had to give allowances for a child for doing what is expected of them? The bills are paid and they live in the same house as I do.

I understand that this varies from household to household, but in the case of my sister and me, my father gave us money for our good grades only when he felt like it; so on the next grades, he gave us nothing. I asked, "Daddy, where is my money?"

He said, "You will get it once you get grown and on your own."

My parents did not let us get comfortable with what belonged to them. Yes, I agree with an inheritance, but it should also be earned.

Spare the Rod, Spoil the Child

Proverbs 13:24, NIV, "Whoever spares the rod hates their children, but the one who loves their children is careful to discipline them."

Some of you will take this scripture and define it like Ms. Trunchbull, the principal from the movie *Matilda* (1996). "You should take the rod and beat the child!" This is what she told Matilda's father when he said Matilda was a difficult child. This is not what I am insinuating. I am defining the rod as the word of God.

Spoiling kids can produce rotten kids. You can never do enough to satisfy them when you prioritize their wants over their needs. Children may want the newest version of gym shoes seen on television when they really need a book to complete a homework assignment. Parents must ask themselves, what is more important for the child's well-being? The wrong decision by the parent can hinder the growth of children into becoming productive adults.

When parents spoil the children, they have a tendency to always expect things and never learn value systems. I once read an article on Fox News (January, 2018) where a single mother gave

49

her young daughter a weekly allowance of $7 a week. From this amount, the mother deducted $5 for rent, utilities, food and water, leaving the child with only $2 to save or spend. The objective of the mother was to teach the child the responsibilities, the value of money, and give the child a glimpse into the real world. In the long run, this strategy will give the child an appreciation for the tremendous discount the parent actually extended.

It's Okay to "Raise Hell!"

Discipline is often painful and never viewed as pleasant.

No discipline seems pleasant at the time, but painful.
Later on, however, it produces a harvest of righteousness
and peace for those who have been trained by it.
(Hebrews 12:11, NIV)

I spoke the word when Mariah got so out of hand, and I thought I was going to lose it the first time she was disobedient. The first incident of disobedience was not the last, but it was the first time I realized beating her was not the answer. I remember my pastor saying in a sermon that God can do more with a person than you can. I knew I needed God's wisdom in dealing with her.

The Lord led me to the book of wisdom which is the book of Proverbs. I had Mariah read one chapter a day for thirty-one days as there are thirty-one chapters. Now to be honest, she did not change or get it right away. Remember, it's about planting seeds. Know this: some kids will enroll themselves into the school of "hard knocks." They are the "I hear you but I'm still going to do it my way" children. It won't give them a pass, but all children are different.

Don't Enable Destructive Behavior

There must be a proper balance needed between verbal reproof and encouragement and the application of corporal punishment as seen in the book of wisdom, Proverbs.

> Foolishness is bound in the heart of a child; but the rod of correction shall drive it far from him. (Proverbs 22:15, NIV)

> Do not withhold discipline from a child; if you punish them with the rod, they will not die. Punish them with the rod and save them from death. (Proverbs 23:13-14, NIV)

> The rod and reproof give wisdom, but a child left to himself brings shame to his mother. Correct your son, and he will give you rest; yes, he will give delight to your soul. (Proverbs 29:15,17, EMP)

There must be a combination of positive instructions, encouragement, and nurturing in conjunction with appropriate punishment. This cannot be overestimated nor discounted.

Kids Appreciate Discipline

I know you are saying, "Really, how could this be?" Through disciplining them, you are trying to teach your children, help them assume responsibility, and internalize your rules and values while maintaining a healthy relationship with them. I worked in an industry where kids came from homes that didn't require discipline. From an undisciplined environment into a disciplined environment, the children would later talk about how it was difficult but very rewarding. Discipline builds your child's character. Parents want their children to grow into independent responsible adults who are respectful, appreciative, mature, with a strong work ethic and moral values.

Your child can possess these traits through discipline and using consequences effectively. Discipline is not always understood at the time by the child; however, later in life it is appreciated. This also becomes a rule of thumb in raising future generations.

Don't punish your children for not being like you. It is probably a good thing they didn't follow in your footsteps. We're not trying to make clones; we just want them to walk in the calling that God has for them. As a parent, it is our responsibility to help our children reach their highest potential, even if it is not what we want for them. We must ask ourselves a few questions about their choices. Is it respectful? Is it morally upright? Is it ethical? If we can answer yes, then we must help guide them into their destiny.

Notes

What scriptures or principles stood out in this chapter?

_____

_____

_____

_____

_____

_____

What will I do to prepare myself and or children as it relates to this chapter?

_____

_____

_____

_____

_____

_____

My prayer is.....

_____

_____

_____

_____

_____

_____

_____

Chapter 5
I Owe You Nothing

Owe nothing to anyone except for your obligation to love
one another. If you love your neighbor, you will fulfill
the requirements of God's law.

—Romans 13:8, NLT

It's okay to say "No!"

This "no" means I have made a decision because I
"know." As my mother has often said, "I have been where you are
trying to go." They are the children, not you.

When did we start fearing our children? At the age of
eighteen, the system or government says that they are grown and
can make their own decisions. So I believe I have the right to say
"No!" Teach them early so you won't be afraid to say it when
they're grown.

My mother never had a problem with telling us no; and
guess what? We did not question it. And if we did, she would say,
"Because I said so!" That was the end of the conversation. We
discuss or explain everything to our kids today.

Child: "Mom, can I have some candy?"

Parent: "No!"

Child: "Why not?"

Parent: "Well, you see, you can't have it because you have
not had dinner;" or, "Candy is not healthy;" or, "Because it's too
late."

Child: "But Mom!"

Enough is enough. You often find yourself going back and forth with your child on a dialogue that is, at most times, unnecessary. We don't have to explain every detail of our "No!" I believe in teachable moments, but every moment does not require explanations at that moment. The answer is *no*, because I *know*.

Don't Become an Enabler

Lack of preparation on your part does not mean an emergency on my part (Author Unknown). As I have already discussed in an earlier chapter, when you have given the tools and or instructions for life, it is now up to them to use those tools. They should not harass you about it after you have given them what they needed. They chose to do things their way and, consequently, ran into problems. They can't expect you to continue bailing them out! Your children will become adults who always expect someone else to work things out for them, even if things went wrong because of their own actions.

Children Today Lack a Sense of Urgency

I have a friend whose daughter we call "old lady," because no matter what she is asked to do, she will take her time doing it. Growing up, I remember when my parents called us, we would answer, "Yes, ma'am," while we were headed their way or following whatever instructions they were screaming our way. Children today are given instructions five or six times, over and over again, before actually doing what we ask them. My son is sometimes guilty of this. He can be occupied with his devices, and when I call, he initially comes and says, "Yes, ma'am," and then backtracks and says, "Hold on, let me finish this" or "Let me pause the game."

My response to him is, "I don't care what you're doing. When I call, you come." When a child puts you on hold, he is showing disrespect for your, "Come now!" This behavior can become worse as they get older. One night, you will tell them to do the dishes after dinner and wake up the next morning to have breakfast, and the dishes are still dirty from the night before.

You can't Worship them; you must Raise them

"Do not turn to idols or make for yourselves any gods of cast metal: I am the Lord your God" (Leviticus 19:4, EVS).

Pastor Jeremy Bell says in an article called *Parents, Stop Idolizing Your Children*, "You may be thinking—correctly—that the Bible teaches children are a blessing from God. Children indeed are a blessing (cf. Psalm 127:3–5). Children are not the problem, and having children is not the problem. However, when we elevate children from a good thing to be celebrated to a god thing to be worshiped, we begin to dip into the dangerous waters of idol worship."

He gives four symptoms of a heart that has idolized children:

Symptom 1: Parents believe their children can do no wrong.

Symptom 2: Parents believe their children have ultimate authority.

Symptom 3: Parents believe their relationship to their children is supreme.

Symptom 4: Parents believe they must sacrifice
everything for their children.

Parents who idolize their children are unable to say the word "No." Instead, they sacrifice everything at the altar of their children. We must repent and place Jesus Christ back on the throne of our hearts.

We must live out our faith through obedience to his authority, not the authority of our children.

Tough Love

Webster defines this as love or affectionate concern expressed in a stern or unsentimental manner (as through discipline), especially to promote responsible behavior.

The womb/nest is, as we mentioned in Chapter 2, considered now as the home, a safe place for them to come back to but not stay. Our now children/young adults feel entitled to the stuff that you worked for. I have a friend whose adult children feel as if they can come home whenever things go bad or even just because they can to avoid real life issues such as bills, groceries, or even employment.

Are you that parent who is always saying, "Here they come again!" Parents who have raised their children and who should be enjoying their empty nest leave the door open and have made it comfortable for them to keep coming back and take the saying "My house is your house" out of context. This is where tough love has to be displayed.

My house is your temporary home. We should practice being a landlord who owns the place but gives you a lease. What I'm saying is when we rent or lease, we understand that the house, apartment, studio/room doesn't belong to us, and that we must either go by the landlord's rules and on how to treat and take care of their property while making it a temporary home and plan on how to get my own.

While we all welcome a visit of a few days from our adult children, we are not looking for extended time without considering a landlord/lessee relationship.

Inheritance—as parents, we work most of our lives acquiring financial savings and material possessions to enjoy and support us when we can no longer work. It is time for me to enjoy the fruits of my labor. I owe you nothing, and this is mine. Once I have died, you inherit what is left.

Notes

What scriptures or principles stood out in this chapter?

_____

_____

_____

_____

_____

_____

What will I do to prepare myself and or children as it relates to this chapter?

_____

_____

_____

_____

_____

_____

My prayer is.....

_____

_____

_____

_____

_____

_____

_____

Chapter 6
Cutting the Cord

Process of Letting Go

When I was a child, I talked like a child, I thought like a child, I reasoned like a child. When I became a man, I put the ways of childhood behind me.
—1 Corinthians 13:11, NIV

Conception to birth is a process, but once you are born, the umbilical cord is cut. The Google definition of *umbilical cord* is a flexible cordlike structure containing blood vessels and attaching a human or other mammalian fetus to the placenta during gestation; the process of carrying or being carried in the womb between conception and birth; pregnancy, incubation: development, maturation; the development of something over a period of time.

"Various Ideas are in the Process of Gestation"

If you trust the gestation process, the word of God and his manual, you should not have a problem cutting the cord.

Physically
Let the Grown be on their Own

When I say grown, I mean an adult person who by virtue of attaining a certain age—generally eighteen—is regarded in the eyes of the law as being able to manage his or her own affairs. If you have done the work and equipped your children with the principles discussed in the previous chapters, then you should not have an issue with letting them be grown.

I remember when Mariah turned eighteen. Every time we went to handle her business affairs, someone would say to me she is eighteen and she has to fill out her own paperwork and handle her own affairs. I remember when she was working at a fast food restaurant after graduating from high school. Her employer suggested the midnight shift. I told her that she could not work that late living in my house. Mariah informed the employer that her parents would not allow her to work those late hours.

The employer's response was, "Why? You are grown (by the way, they kept her schedule the same because they needed her at the job)."

What I'm trying to say is society accepts and demands that you are no longer responsible for them at eighteen years of age. You can be tried in a court of law as an adult if you commit certain crimes.

When you are no longer happy to see them or be around them, and their way is better than your way, it is time to cut the cord. Be reminded that this has nothing to do with your love for the adult children. They have all the answers and will sometimes have the nerve to tell you to let them run their own life. That's a good indication that it is time for you to cut the cord. When you are to the point you're tired of being sick and tired of unappreciative adult children, you must cut the cord or you will become an enabler, depressed, and angry. This can cause bitterness between parent and adult child.

I know someone is going to say this is harsh thinking. But it doesn't mean you love them any less. It is just time has come for them to experience life and apply all you have poured into them. Parents, it is time to watch the fruit grow in their own space and place.

Spiritually
You are not their Savior

Now we see things imperfectly, like puzzling reflections in a 1130 mirror, but then we will see everything with perfect clarity. All that I know now is partial and incomplete, but then I will know everything completely, just as God now knows me completely. (1 Corinthians 13:12, NLT)

And the peace of God which surpasses all understanding, shall keep your hearts, your minds through Christ Jesus. (Philippians 4:7)

When peace like a river attendeth my way,
When sorrows like sea billows roll;
Whatever my lot, Thou hast taught me to say,
It is well, it is well with my soul.
—Horatio G. Spafford

We have done all that has been assigned to us for our children and we should have no regrets. It is now time to give them back to the one who trusted us to raise them, Jesus Christ.

Emotionally and Financially
When they Want or Take More than What they Give

Children come into this world taking. Taking your love, finances, time, and even, sometimes, your sanity. As you raise them and you teach them, tell them love is a two-way streak and you should not be the only one giving something.

There is an old Proverb: "Once a man, and twice a child." The meaning of this is a man is born as a child, grows to adulthood, and consequently enters old age when he deteriorates and reverts to a childish state.

It's okay for them to experience failure. You will wear yourself out trying to fix everything. Trial and error is fundamental for problem solving. If you want your children to become who God wants them to be, then let them fail.

Notes

What scriptures or principles stood out in this chapter?

_____

_____

_____

_____

_____

_____

What will I do to prepare myself and or children as it relates to this chapter?

_____

_____

_____

_____

_____

_____

My prayer is.....

_____

_____

_____

_____

_____

_____

_____

Chapter 7
"Get Out!"

Crossing the Threshold

Crossing of the first threshold echoes the acceptance of the call with physical action, proving that the hero can follow intent with positive action.

Crossing of threshold is a highly symbolic act, such as in the rites of passage of transition to adulthood or the carrying of a bride by a husband over the threshold of their first house. It indicates commitment and change, leaving behind the old and accepting the new.

This is a defining moment in the life of the hero, often the first active decision of responsibility and independence. This is stepping into a bold new world and is often a very scary act, going from the safety of home into an unpredictable and dangerous world, where the rules are different and the cost of failure is high.

Passing the Mantle

Trust God and let your children go. Your child may be destroyed if you keep them home. You may keep them from experiencing their own relationship with God.

But because of His great love for us, God, who is rich in mercy, 1181 made us alive in Christ even when we were dead in transgressions–it is by grace you have been saved. And God raised us up with Christ and seated us with

Him in the heavenly realms in Christ Jesus. (Ephesians 2:4–6, NIV)

Fly, Baby, Fly

Mariah's first flight was when she left for college, and to see her boarding the plane was so real that I was overcome with emotion.

But those who hope in the LORD will renew their strength. They will soar on wings like eagles; they will run and not grow weary, they will walk and not be faint. (Isaiah 40:31, NIV)

Your wings are strong, try them out. You never know you can fly if you don't try. Brothers and sisters, stop thinking like children. In regard to evil be infants, but in your thinking be adults. (1 Corinthians 1198 14:20, NIV)

What used to feed you can't feed you anymore! From Hebrews 5:13-14, "Anyone who lives on milk, being still an infant, is not acquainted with the teachings about righteousness. But solid food is for the mature, who by constant use have trained themselves to distinguish good from evil."
Parents, "Let Go and Let God!"

I am the living bread that came down from heaven. Whoever eats this bread will live forever. This bread is my flesh, which I will give for the life of the world. (John 6:51, NIV)

Watch from a distance and pray, "Be always on the watch, and pray that you may be able to escape all that is about to happen, and that you may be able to stand before the Son of Man." (Luke 21:36)

I have listed below the Merriam-Webster Dictionary definition of *get* and *out*. Why, you may ask? Because I want you to visually see it and mentally and spiritually get it. The words *get* and *out* refer to the parenting principles mentioned in this book. I pray you will be encouraged to utilize practice and enforce the chapters that apply to you. I also share you share this book with someone who has been called to parent or care for children; remember, it takes a village.

The Merriam Webster Dictionary defines the word *get* as:
> a transitive verb;
> to cause to come or to go;
> to cause to move (*"get it out of the house"*);
> to make ready: prepare;
> to prevail on: cause (*"finally got them to tidy their room"*);
> understand (*"he got I was serious"*);
> to establish communication with;
> to succeed in coming or going: to bring or move oneself;
> to make progress;
> to acquire wealth;
> to be able;
> to come to be;
> to succeed in becoming (*"how to get"*);
> to become involved;
> to leave immediately (*"told them to get"*);

Definition of *out*:

> Adverb;
>
> in a direction away from the inside or center;
>
> from among others;
>
> away from home or work;
>
> away from a particular place;
>
> to the point of depletion, extinction, or exhaustion (*"The food ran out"* to completion or satisfaction; *"hear me out"*; *"work the problem out"*);
>
> at the end (*"before the day is out"*);
>
> fly out;
>
> used on a two-way radio circuit to indicate that a message is complete and no reply expected.

Empty Nest

noun;

> household in which one or more parents live after the children have left home.

This is the tailpiece of this book, the part you've been preparing yourself and your child for, and the part that happens after you decide to activate the principles outlined in this book. This is an opportunity to enjoy your life and or even figure out who you are through a life without children.

Grieving Process
It's Normal and it's Okay

From the day Mariah came to live with me, I told her and myself that the goal was for me to get her grown and out. But I must admit it was bittersweet when she finally left for college. It felt strange not having her walking in or out through the door, not having to tell her to clean up the loose strands of hair in the bathroom. One night, I found myself getting up to pray over her while she slept and realized that she was not in there. But guess what? You must not dwell on your grief. Get over it! Life goes on!

Change the environment or setting. Downsize if you are living in a house that is too big or even change the space which the child, now an adult, used to occupy. I homeschool my son, so I changed Mariah's room into a part classroom, part guest room, and part prayer room with a small altar. Whenever Mariah comes to visit, she still has a comfy bed to sleep in; but as I said earlier in the book, you must make it uncomfortable where they want their own.

I watch HGTV and I see parents buying big and huge homes that include rooms for adult children who have left for college. Why? They will spend more time away than they will coming home for spring or winter break.

Invest in you! The word *live* sticks out to me when I look at the definition of *empty nest*. Time to live your life! Well, I have one out and another with at the least thirteen more years before getting to that stage, Lord willing. There are just some things you can't do or have to sacrifice when you are raising and caring for children. Whatever that is or was, now is the time for you to enjoy you. I'm sure God misses that time with you! Travel, make a bucket list of things you've always wanted to do but couldn't. And if you are married, make this the part of your lives when you no longer have to plan a date night, because every night is date night.

Notes

What scriptures or principles stood out in this chapter?

_____

_____

_____

_____

_____

_____

What will I do to prepare myself and or children as it relates to this chapter?

_____

_____

_____

_____

_____

_____

My prayer is.....

_____

_____

_____

_____

_____

_____

_____

Chapter 8
It's Never Too Late

Let us not become weary in doing good, for at the proper time we will reap a harvest if we do not give up.

—Galatians 6:9, NIV

Take Charge
It's Never Too Late; Behavior can be Changed

Do not conform to the pattern of this world, but be transformed by the renewing of your mind. Then you will be able to test and approve what God's will is—his good, pleasing and perfect will. 1284 (Romans 12:2, NIV)

Demand respect, take charge of your space and your place. I was one of the adults who had to return home on several different occasions for many different reasons. But none of them were because I wanted to just be at home. I always had a plan I was working on getting out. You see, my mother had always promised us that she would make sure she had a place for us to return to. My mother never directly discussed getting out of the nest with my sister and me, but she prepared us to be able to leave when the time came. She didn't say "Get out!" But she often used this phrase: "This is my house!"

I know that I'm not the only one who has heard that from a parent. Hearing that, growing up, made me think, "I can't wait to get my own house!" Don't get me wrong, I understand what she meant; and now that I have my own kids, I have said the same thing to them on occasion. Bishop T. D. Jakes mentioned in a sermon I once heard that the eagle makes it uncomfortable for the eaglet to want to stay in the nest once they have sent them out for their trial flight and they return home to get ready to be sent out again to soar on their own.

My mother always had an open door, and I was grateful for it. But there is a saying: "Grown folks can't live in a house together." That's unless they're married, and truth be told, that too is an adjustment in itself.

My husband would say when we had to go home to my mother's before we left for Georgia, "I'm a man who needs to be the king of my own house and your mother is the queen of her house!"

My mother wasn't unbearable to live with, but it was clear it was her house, her ways, her rules. I consider it an issue when grown kids are bluntly disrespectful to their parents, and because they are grown, they feel all of the sudden like they're on the same level as them and can talk to them any kind of way. Some of them even get the notion that they can live in their parents' house and not communicate at all. There are also situations where the adult child comes in and out the house whenever they want, being insensitive to the fact that you the parent/owner may not want or even be use to in and out traffic or would even like for you doors lock in the wee hours of the night. Let's not forget to mention, your losing sleep waiting for them to get home. Also, remind them, This is my HOUSE! If you don't like it, GET OUT!

When parents try and discuss these issues, the grown kids even become verbally abusive, still riding on the notion that they're on their parents' level, debating their rules. If you have kids like these, I suggest you tell them what the elders always said to us and to the other kids they had watched and guided while growing up: the gap in age between you and them had not changed from the time they were born, and no matter how grown they may be, you are still older than them, and they can never outgrow the fact that they should practice some respect.

Get a Plan, and Work the Plan

The plan could be you starting from whatever chapter related to you from reading this book. The plan can also be assisting your adult child with a plan to "Get Out!" Refer to the m.wikihow.com post *How to Get Your Adult Children to Move Out*.

Don't give up!

Jesus looked at them intently and said, "Humanly speaking, it is impossible. But with God everything is possible." (Matthew 19:26, NLT)

New Beginnings = A Fresh Start

"Never regret anything that has happened in your life, it cannot be change, undone or forgotten. So take it as a lesson learned and move on" (Author Unknown). No regrets, just lessons. No worries, just acceptance. No expectations, just gratitude. Life is too short. There are going to be times when you will start a rule and will break a rule. You will be inconsistent and then become consistent, but know that every day is a knew day. I've been a parent to children that God has trusted me with for over twenty-five years; know that it wasn't always an easy task. "But

God!" The fruit of your labor will be rewarding. Below are scriptures that will encourage you into your new beginnings:

Remember not the former things, nor consider the things of old. Behold, I am doing a new thing; now it springs forth, do you not perceive it? I will make a way in the wilderness and rivers in the desert. (Isaiah 43:18–9, ESV)

See, I will create new heavens and a new earth. The former things will not be remembered, nor will they come to mind. (Isaiah 65:17, NIV)

The steadfast love of the Lord never ceases; his mercies never come to an end; they are new every morning; great is your faithfulness. (Lamentations 3:22–23, ESV)

And when they come there, they will remove from it all its detestable things and all its abominations. And I will give them one heart, and a new spirit I will put within them. I will remove the heart of stone from their flesh and give them a heart of flesh. (Ezekiel 11:18–19, ESV)

And I will give you a new heart, and a new spirit I will put within you. And I will remove the heart of stone from your flesh and give you a heart of flesh. (Ezekiel 36:26, ESV)

Or don't you know that all of us who were baptized into Christ Jesus were baptized into his death? We were therefore buried with him through baptism into death in order that, just as Christ was raised from the dead through the glory of the Father, we too may live a new life. (Romans 6:3–4, NIV)

Therefore, if anyone is in Christ, he is a new creation. The old has passed away; behold, the new has come. (2 Corinthians 5:17, ESV)

To put off your old self, which belongs to your former manner of life and is corrupt through deceitful desires, and to be renewed in the spirit of your minds, and to put on the new self, created after the likeness of God in true righteousness and holiness. (Ephesians 4:22–24, ESV)

Brothers and sisters, I do not consider myself yet to have taken hold of it. But one thing I do: Forgetting what is behind and straining toward what is ahead, I press on toward the goal to win the prize for which God has called me heavenward in Christ Jesus. (Philippians 3:13–14, NIV)

Do not lie to each other, since you have taken off your old self with its practices and have put on the new self, which is being renewed in knowledge in the image of its Creator. (Colossians 3:9–10 NIV)

Blessed be the God and Father of our Lord Jesus Christ! According to his great mercy, he has caused us to be born again to a living hope through the resurrection of Jesus Christ from the dead. (1 Peter 1:3, ESV)

He will wipe away every tear from their eyes, and death shall be no more, neither shall there be mourning, nor crying, nor pain anymore, for the former things have passed away." And he who was seated on the throne said, "Behold, I am making all things new." Also he said, "Write this down, for these words are trustworthy and true. (Revelation 21:4–5, ESV)

Pray, Pray, Pray!

Notes

What scriptures or principles stood out in this chapter?

_____

_____

_____

_____

_____

_____

_____

What will I do to prepare myself and or children as it relates to this chapter?

_____

_____

_____

_____

_____

_____

_____

My prayer is.....

_____

_____

_____

_____

_____

_____

_____

_____

More Praise for Get Out! and Lorene Price Henderson

My wife has spoken this book into existence. She kept saying in 2017, "I'm going to write a book!" and, wow! Here it is! Get Out! is a great book with so much vital information. The book speaks of parenting love, life, and that importance of discipline and having a relationship with God. I'm so proud of you, baby, may God bless you on this journey.

—Simeon Henderson, husband

I remember when my aunt told me about her writing this book, and I'm glad to see that she has completed it. I'm sure I can use it in helping me to raise my daughter, just like many others will with raising their kids.

—Ashley Willis, niece

Wow! Lorene you did it! With much prayer and meditation, you were able to complete this God-given task. I am so proud of you, because I know your spirit. I've seen you struggle, but you always called on God, and the outcome was blessed. I see more books being birthed and your labor pains will be lessened. May our God continue to bless your ministry.

—Pastor Debra Wadlington House

Get Out! is a must read for parents of this millennial generation. Lorene takes "privilege comes with responsibility" to a new level. As an enabler of adult children, I wish she had written this book years ago!

—T'vet Coates

Congratulations, Lorene, on accomplishing your goal of becoming an author. Your hard work and determination has paid off. We know this is going to impact and inspire many. The best is yet to come.

—Keith and Patreasa Haywood

Lorene, finally all your God-given, Holy Ghost inspired wisdom on paper. Over the past twenty-five plus years of our friendship, you have always proven to defy the status quo and challenge everyone you come in contact with to become a better version of themselves. As an author, I'm so excited that the world get to meet this godly woman who is inspiring courageous, unique, loving, and anointed. This book will cause people to look at truth and decide to do what's right, because it concerns their family. I love you and I declare that you are blessed, and may God's favor rest on this first of many other books to come.

—Irlande Marius

Congrats, Lorene! You are a wife, mother, and now an author. You have inspired me, and I know this book will do the same for so many others.

—Grace E. Gregory

Lorene has been a moral compass for her friends and family. Her love for God and youth has inspired her to share her life experiences with the world. *Get Out!* is a practical guide to implementing what the word of God says: "Train up a child in the way he should go and when he is old he will not depart from it" (Proverbs 22:6, NIV). I'm so excited about Lorene's book release as it will be a blessing to many for generations to come.

The wisdom and knowledge expressed in this book is genuine, and I've been blessed to see this unfold throughout my life as well. "No discipline seems pleasant at the time, but painful. Later on, however, it produces a harvest of righteousness and peace for those who have been trained by it" (Hebrews 109 12:11, NIV). It may not have always been easy for either parent or child, but with God, the deed was done. "Like an eagle that stirs up its nest and hovers over its young, that spreads its wings to catch them and carries them aloft" (Deuteronomy 32:11, NIV). So very proud of you and seeing your visions coming to life!

—Kirsten C. Brooks

"The joy of the Lord is your strength." You put your faith to work... I am truly proud of the outcome.

—Sarah Kuenyefu

Almost twenty years ago, I met Lorene, and twenty years later, she has been the same—always consistent, always loving, but didn't take nonsense. She was affectionately named an "aunt" of mine, the person you could share things with that you couldn't share with your parent, but she could still check you like a parent. I've always appreciated her wisdom, knowledge, and support. I know this book will be a blessing to all who pick it up, just like Lorene has been a blessing to me.

—Jonnice Clanton

As a rising senior in college, this book is not only important but necessary for me to successfully transition into the next chapter in life. My family has always viewed establishing and maintaining a relationship with God as the fulcrum point of our success. My aunt has reinforced this notion in this powerful work of art. The mere completion of this book shows the power of faith. All that she speaks on in this book are all personal nuggets of wisdom she has used to advise me on my personal journey. I am so proud of all that you have accomplished, and I cannot wait for you to receive all of the blessing that God has in store for you! Love you to the moon and back!

—Nia Gipson, niece

There are many evangelicals and there are many wise parents offering practical advice on child-rearing. But only a small intersection of those two groups have attempted to build a sound connection between living by the Word and navigating these modern times as a parent. Lorene is among this rare breed of preacher-writers. She has written this book with the deep conviction that God himself put this book in her heart, and it's her responsibility to bring it forth to the world. Here, she effortlessly and powerfully cites the parts of the Bible that can arm parents and mentors with much-needed wisdom on how to raise their young faithful, and she gives solid advice rooted in her own life experiences, teeming with understanding of the current social culture without compromising her Christian values.

—Iris Orpi, poet, novelist, and screenwriter

I have the distinction and honor of being best friends with Lorene for over thirty years. As the perpetual writer (with Lorene the talker) in this sisterhood, I am overjoyed to see my friend take the leap of faith to write and release this book. Because of her obedience and willingness to respond to God's gentle nudge, as well as the courage to step out into a world in which she was both unfamiliar and unsure, God has certainly placed His favor on this project. A longtime advocate for children and a champion for the underdog with an appetite for community outreach, Lorene uses her hands-on approach and life experiences to craft a poignant and beautifully written book for those who parent and the children that they love. Anyone who takes on the role of interacting with and pouring into the life of children who cross their pathway in life will benefit from this book. As the mother of five children who currently range in age from thirteen to thirty, I can attest to the importance of having tools to assist in the rearing of whole, God-fearing, loving, responsible children with a biblical foundation. This book is a great resource because Lorene pairs biblical truths with practical ideas to produce a plan of action which is both realistic and attainable. Whatever the stage of life of the child, the reader can jump right into any chapter to address their concern. Congratulations to my friend on this, the first of many books she will write to bless the kingdom of God and his people.

—Valerie A. Howard, author of *Sassy*

What an amazing work God has birthed through you my sister and friend. After twenty plus years of friendship, I have to say that you are continuing to evolve. This is a work that has clearly been in the making for years and it's so purposeful and needed in this day and time. I thank God for you and I am looking forward to the next one. Love you!

—Guineivere Thomas, educator

Made in the USA
Columbia, SC
02 April 2019